HIDEN HITORI SHUGYO

剣術秘伝独修行

JAPANESE SWORDFIGHTING:
SECRETS OF SOLO TRAINING

BY SENEN

PUBLISHED 1799

TRANSLATED BY ERIC SHAHAN

The cover illustration is from a 1636 edition of *The Chronicle of Yoshitsune* which tells the story of Minamoto no Yoshitsune 源義経 (1159~1189.) In this scene Yoshitsune is being taught Kenjutsu by a Tengu mountain goblin.

Translator's Introduction

This book is called *Kenjutsu Hiden Hitori Shugyo* 剣術秘伝独修行 *Japanese Swordfighting: Secrets of Solo Kenjutsu Training*. The introduction was written in "early winter" of Kansei 10 (1798) and it was published in "early winter" of the 11th year of Kansei (1799) and republished the following year in Kansei 12 (1800) in Kyoto. The author is a man named Senen 蒨園 which is probably a penname. One edition of the book has a notation on the spine saying the author is Uno Sanzo Nyudo Kosai Sensei 宇野三蔵入道耕斎先生, which could be Senen's real name. In the book Senen states he is 72 years old at the time of writing, meaning he was born around 1726, a hundred years after the end of the Warring States era.

Japanese Swordfighting: Secrets of Solo Kenjutsu Training is two volumes long, the first volume is titled *General Remarks* and is eighteen pages long. The first chapter also contains some illustrations of basic sword stances and attacks.

The second volume is titled *Secret Teachings* and is thirteen pages long.

Throughout the book the author cites numerous Chinese sources. The names of the books and authors will be recorded as they are known in Japanese and footnotes will give the Kanji and Chinese reading of the name with additional information.

Sentences in *italics* represent the author quoting someone however it is not clear what the source is.

The section titles are all by the translator.

The extremely rare original document is reprinted in its entirety at the end of the book. The book proceeds Japanese style, so the first page of the Japanese edition is at the end of this book, and it proceeds right to left.

ERIC SHAHAN

HIDEN HITORI SHUGYO

剣術秘伝独修行

JAPANESE SWORDFIGHTING: SECRETS OF SOLO TRAINING

BY SENEN

PUBLISHED 1799

TRANSLATED BY ERIC SHAHAN

Kenjutsu Hiden Hitori Shugyo
剣術秘伝独修行
Secrets of Japanese Swordfighting
A Guide to Solo Training
Book 1
Soron
総論
Overview

Introduction

自序

或雖曰古人有謂也人非生而知之者
于此師其為惑終不解矣諸藝皆然矣
而予編輯修行者宣困随平予對曰物
研術養蘊推求其末歷即是也末至于
妻予宜有而森羅萬像不可得而數也
卻術之術玄流多端則其業運而
萬別而其来一也者所固有之者
此謂父子不傳也是以每人有下流磨
如人面之同而各異也此其姓所龍以
異於役其好之是效以傳之彼非所有
而傳之終身不成也鳴呼感乳姓者不
可矯也惟能住欖不蕩稽外其行全美
名之曰欖修行月
寛政戊午之初冬舊園謹識

師一筆之玄

Introduction

Some people say, *The ancients taught that no one has any skills at birth, so if you do not study with a teacher, you will remain lost.* This is true of all the arts. However, should we consider a person who trains on his own to be stubborn and uneducated? It is said,

There is always a history of things, but if you delve deep enough into it you will find it started from nothing at all.

The arts are all like that.

The world is nothing, but it is the source of all things. All things in the universe must be obtained and do not simply appear. As for the creation of something from nothing, there is no way to count all things in the universe and it is impossible to obtain all things. The same is true of swordsmanship.

Since there are many branches of Kenjutsu schools, there are a thousand different techniques though, in the end they each return to one principle. However, a person with his own style can have something unique. For example, it is said that the son does not transmit the same teachings his father passed to him. This is why it is said that each person has their own unique technique. In addition, while the faces of people are more or less the same, they are still different from each other. This is where your nature lies. This is why we are different from each other.

Thus we all have different likes and dislikes. This is what I wish to teach. If you try and teach what another has learned, you, yourself, will not be able to transmit your unique nature throughout your life. Ah, I realize this is all a bit confusing. The nature of the person cannot be corrected. If you are able to remain steadfast in your commitment to training Kenjutsu, you will be able to find success even training on your own.

This is what is meant by the word Hitori Shugyo, Solo Intensive Training.

Written in early winter of the 10th year of Kansei (1798)
By Senen

Japanese Swordfighting: Secrets of Solo Kenjutsu Training
Book 1 : Overview

劍術秘傳獨修行卷之上
總論

東都　舊園述

剣術秘伝独修行 *Kenjutsu Hiden Hitori Shugyo*
Secrets of Japanese Swordfighting: A Guide to Solo Training
Book 1 総論 *Soron* Overview

There are many schools of Kenjutsu and all of the founders of these schools were famous expert swordsman and thus later generations preserved their teachings. Therefore, every school of sword is good and you cannot say that any of them are bad. Any person who devotes themselves exclusively to Shugyo, intensive training, will become an expert swordsman. You often hear people disparaging this school or criticizing that school while failing to realize their own lack of experience. Further, while doing this they will also begin to harbor doubts about[1] their own teacher and end up quitting one school after another. This is called Hen-Ryu 変流, changing schools. This type of person will never become a true Kenjutsu expert.

While this applies to all arts, you should approach martial arts training with clear intent. If you do not you will not be able to master a single technique. Long ago in China there was a Shogun named Ri Ko who was out hunting.[2] He mistook a large rock for a tiger hiding

---

[1] Kogi 狐疑 This word is two Kanji Fox + Doubt. A fox, considered to be a magical creature, is one full of doubt.

[2]

Li Guang 李 広(184 ~ 119 BC) was a Chinese military general of the Western Han dynasty.

in the grass, and shot an arrow at it. Approaching the spot, he found that his arrow had lodged deep into the rock. Later, Ri Ko tried shooting an arrow at a rock, but it did not penetrate.

The reason the arrow did not penetrate the second time is because initially the Shogun was absolutely sure what he was shooting at was a tiger crouching in the grass, not a rock. This is why his arrow sank so deep into the rock that only the nock of the arrow could be seen. Later, when Ri Ko tried to shoot a rock, he failed because he no longer had his initial conviction as to the nature of his target.

Similarly, you should approach Kenjutsu training with the same, pure first intention. That being said, you cannot focus solely on your state of mind when training as described in books like Takuan's *Military Strategy and Swordfighting*.[3] This is not going to help you and will likely muddle your head which will make you useless. While it is said *Waza wa Ki Kara Umareru*, or Techniques are born from spirit, you must first learn a technique before learning how Ki, your spirit, should be applied. Over the course of many training sessions, you will become able to unify *Ki to Waza*, or both Sprit and Technique. However, achieving this requires an incredible amount of hard training.

The amount of effort required to unify your body and mind requires that you train until your bones turn to powder and your flesh is rent asunder. The best way to achieve this is to receive instruction directly from a teacher of the art. No matter what art you are seeking to pursue, having a teacher is best, without one you will be simply doing trial and error, meaning your ability will not progress.

---

[3] This is referring to Takuan Soho's book commonly known in English as *Immovable Wisdom*. The book was published under various titles in the Edo Era. It was written in the early 17th century by Takuan, a Zen monk. In the book Takuan compares the mindset necessary for Zen enlightenment with the mindset of a swordsman.

Yoshida Kenko wrote in *Essays in Idleness* about a Monk who had set out to pray at Ishi Kiyomizu Hachimangu[4], Rock by the Pure Water of the God of War Temple, atop Otokoyama "Men's Mountain." However, the monk mistakenly paid his respects at a temple located at the foot of the mountain and then returned home without having achieved his intended goal. Yoshida writes that the reason for this error was he had no one to teach him the proper way.

That being said, the purpose of this book is to outline a method for solo Kenjutsu training. The reason you must train alone could be because of work, your position, or the fact that there are no sword instructors or training partners where you live. Also some people may desire to train in the sword arts but are unable to due to financial reasons. It is for these people that I have written this book.

Frankly, without an instructor you will never achieve success. By saying this I am no doubt going to draw criticism, since this is ostensibly a book about solo training, however, allow me to explain. Initially, a person may be interested in the way of the sword and, out of a pure desire to learn, worked fervently until he achieved success, making Kenjutsu part of his body. So since his motivations were pure and he worked diligently, many will believe that it must have been due to god's grace that he achieved success.

When the Chinese philosopher and politician Kan Igo, who lived in the State of Qui, was serving as prime minister her wrote,

Think on it and then recall it, then consider it again. If you find yourself at a loss, pray to a fierce god to show you the way.[5]

---

[4] Yoshida Kenko 吉田兼好(1283~1350) *Tsurezuregusa* 徒然草 *Essays in Idleness*. This temple, which is located in Kyoto, is dedicated to Hachiman 八幡 the god of archery and war. Hachiman means "eight banners" referring Emperor Ojin 応神天皇 who ruled in the 3rd~4th centuries. Ojin was known as as "Yahata-no-kami" meaning "Kami of Eight Banners", referring to the eight heavenly banners that signaled his birth. He is also known as Yumiya Hachiman 弓矢八幡 Bow and Arrow Eight Banners.

[5] Guan Zhong 管仲 (720 ~ 645) was a Chinese philosopher and politician. His philosophy is recorded in a book called *Guanzi* 管子 though it was not written by Guan Zhong himself.

This sort of thing will only occur if you have a pure intent and are making a diligent effort. However, just thinking that you must train is not enough to make a person an expert, even if they are a god.

In the *Analects* by the great Confucius, we find the line,

Going a day without food, going a night without sleep as you ponder something is a complete waste of time. Instead take action.[6]

In the history of Kenjutsu you hear of people receiving instruction from a fierce god, or maybe they are visited in a dream by a divine being. However, the reason such an apparition visits you is because you have a true sense of purpose and have devoted yourself wholly to your pursuit. The deity has sensed your commitment and has offered assistance. Thus, that divine insight is the result of your own diligence and effort. Anyone who thinks they cannot put any effort into learning and just pray to the gods to master an art is a delusional fool.

When I speak of divine inspiration, this is not a deity appearing before you every day to teach, nor is it likely that a divine being will appear in your dreams nightly. Instead, after a long period of intense effort you might receive a single lesson that serves to crystallize or give great insight into some concept you have been struggling to comprehend. Clearly, a single lesson or a single dream is not going

---

[6] Confucius (551-479 BCE), *The Analects* - 15
The Master said, I have been the whole day without eating, and the whole night without sleeping:-occupied with thinking. It was of no use. A better plan is to learn.
                                   -Translated by James Legge (1815-1897)

The Master said, Once, lost in my thoughts, I went a whole day without eating and a whole night without sleeping. I got nothing out of it, and would have been better off devoting the time to learning.
                        -Translated by Roger T. Ames and Henry Rosemont, Jr
                                                                        1998
Another similar line, also by Confucius:
The Master said, Learning without thought is labor lost; thought without learning is perilous.   -Legge

to enable you to master an art you have no real experience with. If you do not make an effort to learn, then it is impossible for you to be adept at any art.

Sword Stances

There are many different schools of sword, and each school focuses on a different Kamae. Some schools focus on Jodan, upper stance, while others place great importance on Seigan, mid-level stance, or even Irimi, moving your body directly against your opponent. This focus is because it is the specialty of the founder of the school, who then passes those lessons onto his students. These are actually the founding sword master's Tekuri, distinctive ways of fighting and handling sword. [7] The Tekuri is also reflected in the name of the school.

This doesn't just apply to Kenjutsu but also to calligraphy and other fine arts. The way the founder of a school of calligraphy wrote with his brush can still be seen in his works and is also reflected in the name of his school.

This might just be my own opinion, but being able to pass on an ability that is innate to you, onto another person, who is not a direct descendant of you, is the definition of Ryugi, School of Art. From the perspective of an outsider, the way a certain teacher instructs at his school may seem wrong, however since that method is one that most often leads to that teacher's victory, then that is the method that teacher favors.

If you are at the level of one who instruct, you should be willing to discover within your students what each excels at, and then seek to aid them in developing that aspect. Forcing your students to learn your preferred methodology, one they may be inherently poor at, instead of guiding them to develop their innate strengths, will not enable your students to excel. In the end, students taught in such a way will probably quit training or change to a new teacher.

---

[7] Tekuri 手僻 or Tekuse. These days the word Kuse 癖 refers to a "bad habit" however in this era the word refers to the distinctive style of a martial artist, fine artist or craftsman.

The Chinese philosopher Moshi also discusses this topic.

When dealing with a simple problem people overthink it, making it difficult. [8]

This is the same thing I am trying to describe. With regards to learning Kenjutsu, a person who can discover the innate ability in another person and develop that potential into a practical skill is a person that can be described as a great teacher. This topic will be explained more fully in the second volume. Please read that volume carefully.

There is a saying from the Ekikyo that goes,

Do not forget about chaotic times and peaceful ones. [9]

Therefore it is important to devote yourself to regular Kenjutsu training, even in this time of peace. As a Samurai, if you are not trained in Kenjutsu and your Lord or your family come under attack, even if you are able to face off against the attacker, you are likely to be seriously injured. Not only that, but you may also not be able to succeed in protecting your Lord or your family from danger. This would mean that you have failed both in your official duty to protect your lord and your filial duty to protect your family. You would no doubt receive a sharp rebuke. Would you not feel greatly ashamed in such a situation?

---

[8] Mencius 孟子(372~289 BC). The full quote is as follows,
道在爾而求諸遠 事在易而求諸難 人人親其親 長其長而天下平
It is curious that people choose the longer route when a shorter route exists. When dealing with a simple problem they overthink it, making it difficult. Each and every person should cherish their parents and honor their ancestors, everything under the sky would be peaceful.
[9] The book is more commonly known as the I-Ching 易経.

The Classic of Filial Piety states,[10]

The first step in filial duty is not to injure the body given to you by your mother and father.

Since the purpose of Kenjutsu is to protect the body and not allow it to become injured, it is necessary to train diligently. If you are sent into battle, failing to fight with bravery is to ignore your filial duty. This was also reiterated by Soshi.[11]

---

[10] From *The Classic of Filial Piety* 孝經 written in the 3rd ~4th century BC by an unknown author.
身體髮膚 受之父母 不敢毀傷 孝之始也
Full quote:

The Master said, "(It was filial piety.) Now filial piety is the root of (all) virtue, and (the stem) out of which grows (all moral) teaching. Sit down again, and I will explain the subject to you. Our bodies - to every hair and bit of skin - are received by us from our parents, and we must not presume to injure or wound them. This is the beginning of filial piety.

-Legge

The four Kanji *Shintai Happu* 身體髮膚 refers to the body, hair and skin you received from your parents.
[11] Zeng Shen 曾子(505~435 BC) a Chinese philosopher and disciple of Confucius. The quote is not included.

In order to develop your bravery, you must study the way of the sword. The Shogun Seki Nanto of the Ming Dynasty famously said,

Through the study of Kenjutsu your liver will become fat.[12]

Martial Arts Training

Samurai are fond of many martial arts including archery, horse riding, spear fighting, fighting with a halberd, Jujutsu and Torite, or arresting and tying techniques. However, no matter how high or low a Samurai's station may be, he is wearing two swords on his belt. This means the first thing he will rely on in a fight is his knowledge of Kenjutsu.

The word Bushi, meaning warrior, is another word for Samurai. If we break down the first Kanji in Bushi 武士, the Kanji "Bu" 武 we find that it is comprised of two parts Hoko 戈 meaning halberd, and Todomeru 止 meaning stop. However, many Samurai feel that the Kenjutsu training they have spent their life doing is not something that will benefit them. However, they are not aware of the fact that by training diligently over the course of many years they have unknowingly received divine protection and are therefore truly blessed.[13]

Bringing order to disorder and making calm what was violent is the benevolent duty of Bu 武 the way of the warrior. However, your abilities should not be used to benefit yourself. Using violence in a moment of anger to injure or kill a person will only result in you

---

[12] Qi Jiguang 戚継光 (1528 ~ 1588) His courtesy name was Nanto 南塘. Qi is famous for the military manual *New Treatise on Military Efficiency* 紀効新書 which was read in Japan during this era. The liver is said to be the source of bravery, so "making it fat" means to make it sturdier therefore "making you braver." Conversely if *Your Liver is Chilled* 肝を冷やす it means "to be scared to death."

[13] Samurai Myori 侍冥利 Describes a Samurai that waits and waits for the benefit of his long years of intensive training and finally becomes unexpectedly enlightened. Also known as Myori no Bushi 冥利の武士

destroying yourself. This would be the very epitome of dishonor, affecting both your lord and your parents as there is no way any merit can come from such a killing.

You should never disparage another school. While this applies to any art is it particularly important for those training martial arts. No matter what school you look at, they all have passed down an important lesson.

The people that are part of that school very much feel like their school is better while this school and its members feel that their school has the most effective techniques. Then as they continue to argue, both schools get into a fight, sometimes resulting in an unfortunate loss of life which only serves to damage not only the reputation of the school, but that of the head teacher. Thus you should heed this warning regarding talking about other schools.

Soji said,

If I stand in the center of a sphere, there is no separation between yes and no, myself and another.[14]

How to Learn

After you join a school, if you devote yourself entirely to training respectfully and diligently in accordance with your teacher's instruction, you will, eventually, become stronger and more skilled than your teacher. On the other hand if you begin to think, "This school is not very interesting or, "That school over there seems to be a lot more effective," and use that as a pretext to quit and join another group you will find that you mind will become confused. Since you have not committed yourself, you end up not learning any school of sword completely.

If you have devoted yourself to fully mastering what a certain school of sword contains then you have developed yourself to a level that will allow you to absorb the lessons of any other school of sword you choose to learn from. However, if you do decide to visit another school, the purpose would only be to participate at a learner, not to

---

[14] Zhuang Zhou 莊子(369 ~ 286 BC) a Chinese philosopher.

engage in duels. People that are uncertain in their abilities and seek to conceal that fact do not like to be taught.

As Confucius said,

If I am walking with two others, invariably one of them will teach me something.[15]

You often hear about someone having a book called *Yoshitsune's Tiger Scroll* that contains many haphazard and poorly explained secret teachings. If you unroll it, you will find may illustrations of the Buddha and other deities, however there will be absolutely nothing in about Kenjutsu. In short, an utterly pointless document.

The story goes that Minamoto Yoshitsune[16] was given a military strategy and swordfighting document by a man named Kiichi Hogen,[17] who was a literary man as well as a martial artist.

---

15 *The Analects* Chapter 21.

The Master said, 'When I walk along with two others, they may serve me as my teachers. I will select their good qualities and follow them, their bad qualities and avoid them.

- Legge

[16] Minamoto Yoshitsune 源義経 (1159 ~ 1189) was a military commander in the late Heian Era and probably the most famous Samurai commander.

[17] Kiichi Hogen 鬼一法眼 is a legendary Japanese monk and warrior who appears in the second volume of *The Record of Yoshitsune* 義経記 which was written in the 14th century. Hogen is a honorific title for a monk, meaning "One who sees the law (of Buddhism)" Kiichi means "First Demon."

The book Yoshitsune was given was called *The Rikuto : The Six Weapon Storage Bags*.[18] In the title of this book the Kanji *To* 韜 refers to a military secret.[19] The book is divided into the following chapters:

1. Civil Strategy 文韜: Organizing in order to prepare for battle.
2. Military Strategy 武韜: Assessing your state of readiness before battle and strategies to destabilize the opposing state.
3. Dragon Strategy 龍韜: Describes how to organize the military.
4. Tiger Strategy 虎韜: Battle strategy for fighting on flat land.
5. Leopard Strategy 豹韜: Fighting on difficult terrain as well as offensive and defensive weapons.
6. Dog Strategy 犬韜: How to use mobile infantry.

Unfortunately, fortune tellers have gotten hold of the Tiger Strategy chapter and created a Tora no Maki, Tiger Scroll,[20] and published it with the intent of confusing people. You should place

---

[18] *Rikuto-Sanryaku* 六韜三略 This refers to two books by Lu Shang, who lived in the 11th century BC. Rikuto, or *The Six Secret Teachings* and Sanryaku, or *The Three Strategies*.

Rikuto : The Six Weapon Storage Bags
(The Kanji To 韜 refers to a bag used to store swords or bows.)
Sanryaku: The Three Strategies
Jorykau 上略 Upper Strategy: Aquire talented people as you need them while administering your land carefully.
Churyaku 中略 Middle Strategy: Plan your strategy according to the necessities of the situation and organize your government and coordinate how each part of your organization responds.
Geryaku 下略 Lower Strategy: Regarding how to rule your country and make effective use of your administrators.
[19] The Kanji To 韜 in general refers to a bag used to store swords or bows. The author states in this case it more like "secret technique."
[20] Tora no Maki 虎の巻 Has become a sort of catch all meaning "this scroll will tell you everything you need to know about (some topic.)"

no stock in that book. I trust that anyone of the status of a Samurai would not be tempted to read or place any trust in such a book. Placing any faith in such a book will prevent you from achieving victory.

A man named Sun Tzu said,

The clever combatant imposes his will on the enemy, but does not allow the enemy's will to be imposed on him.[21]

An example of this principle being applied by the Samurai Kusunoki Masashige[22] is described in the *Record of Future Events*[23] held in Shitenno Temple in Osaka as well as in the song Minamoto no Yoshitsune ordered his agents to sing at Usa Hachiman Shrine in Oita Prefecture. In both cases the famous Samurai used techniques to increase their sides fighting spirit while sewing doubt in their

---

[21] Sun Tzu *The Art of War* Translated by Lionel Giles.

[22] Kusunoki Masashige 楠木正成 (1294 ~ 1336) was a Japanese samurai of the Kamakura period remembered as the ideal of Samurai loyalty.

[23] *The Miraiki* 未来記 "Record of Future Events" is an apocryphal book allegedly written by Prince Shotoku 聖徳太子(574 ~ 622 AD.) It contains a great deal of *Shumatsuronteki* 終末論的 "end of the world predictions." In the Edo Era, many documents related to the Miraiki were discovered, however most are considered to be forgeries. Some of these were published titled 皇太子未来記未然本紀 *Future Record of the Crown Prince Foretelling of Future Events*.

One of the entries is a follows,

Two hundred years after my death a virtuous emperor will build a great city here (Kyoto.) There will be many wars, but the city will prosper for a thousand years. After that a black dragon will appear and the capital city will be moved to the east. Two hundred years after that a Kuhanda 鳩槃荼, or a demon with large testicles believed to drain people of their vitality, will appear and sully the city. The capital city will then be split into eight parts, one parent city and seven children cities.

adversaries. This is what is meant by Sun Tzu's quote, *The clever combatant imposes his will on the enemy, but does not allow the enemy's will to be imposed on him.*

What Yoshitsune did was send a group of men to Usa Hachiman Shrine. The men made their way to the interior of the shrine and read a song.

God can't do anything about the hard things in the world, but what are you praying for with all your heart?

While they chanted this song, enemy soldiers of the Heike clan were paying their respects outside the shrine. The sound of the fearful song echoing from inside the shrine threw the Heike soldiers into a panic and some fled in their distress, abandoning their duty while others drowned themselves. This eventually led to the complete destruction of the Heike clan. This is an example of how a good Shogun will control people, a foolish shogun will be controlled by people.

In the *Taiheiki a Chronicle of Medieval Japan* there is an episode that takes place at Temple of the Four Heavenly Kings in 1330. Kusunoki Masashige visits the temple and requests to read the *Miraiki Record of Future Events*. He uses that information to his advantage.

Also, I cannot recall exactly when this occurred, however Masashige was in a battle and ended up fighting hand to hand with an opponent. His opponent managed to take Masashige to the ground and was readying to decapitate him. Masashige looked the Samurai in the eye and said, "Do you know the proper way to take the head of a general?" Masashige's opponent, momentarily puzzled, lost his concentration and Masashige was able to flip the man off and cut him down. This is an important lesson for any swordsman.

Length of the Sword

Samurai all carry swords, but I would like to talk about sword length. There are some people who prefer longer swords and some people who prefer shorter ones. I have heard the arguments from both sides and do not think there is a definitive conclusion about whether a longer sword or a shorter sword is better. Thus it cannot be said that "a longer sword is better" or that "a shorter sword is a disadvantage." For example, if your opponent is less skilled than you are, it does not matter if your sword is long or short, he will pose no threat to you. However, if your opponent is more skilled than you, then a longer sword will get in your way, while a shorter sword will not allow you to reach your opponent. Thus, no matter which sword you use, you will be defeated. [24]

As a general guideline, to find a sword that matches your body, hold the handle with your right hand just below the Tsuba, hand guard. Allow your arm to hang naturally at your side, and if the tip of the sword is just shy of scraping the ground, then that blade is a good match for you. While this may differ for some people, please consider this to be a general rule. That being said different rules

---

24

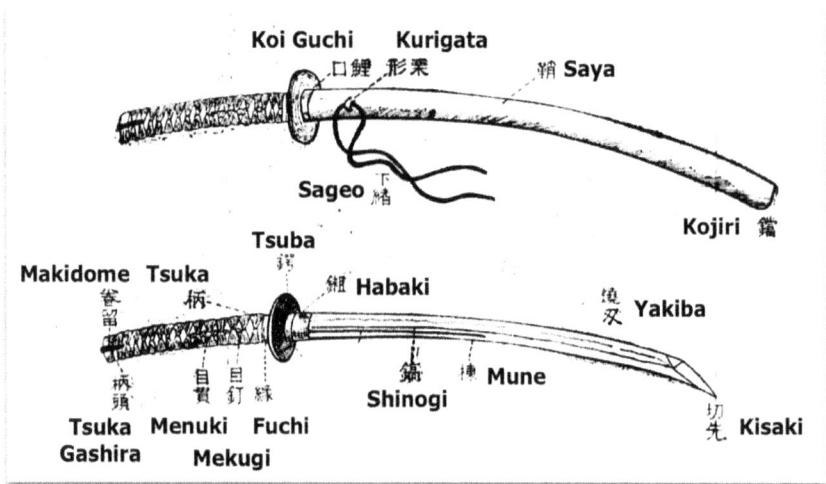

Diagram of a Katana from a pre-World War II Katori Shinto School of sword book.

apply when you are talking about using Nodachi, field swords, with blade lengths over three Shaku, 90 centimeters/35 inches.[25]

Scabbard and Fittings

The fittings as well as the scabbard of each sword should be reserved in style and should not be flashy. Durable fittings and scabbards are best. It is best if the tang of the blade of your sword extends all the way to the pommel. If the tang is too short, your sword's balance will be poor and the handle of your sword might break.

---

[25]

Illustrations of Nodachi "Field Sword" (right) and Itomaki Tachi "Thread Wrapped Handle Sword" (left.) From An Illustrated Guide to 200 Weapons 武器萌図. By Kobayashi Sukemichi 小林祐猷 published 1848.

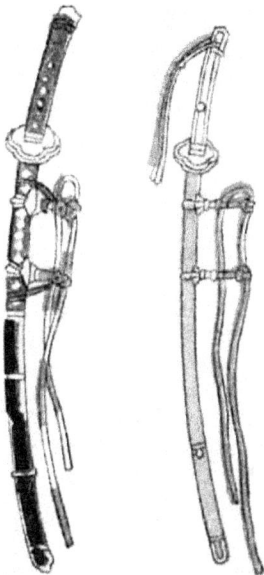

糸巻太刀 いとまきたち　野劔 のだち

Handle

If the handle of your sword is too thick, then you will have trouble handling it deftly and you will be in danger of an opponent knocking it from your hands.

Menuki

There are many people who favor Gyaku Menuki, reversed Menuki. Note that the term Tachi Menuki refers to something else. Long ago the Menuki was meant to cover the Mekuki, preventing it from slipping out. However nowadays they are not placed above the Mekugi and are completely decorative and are just used to show off, so they serve no real purpose.[26]

26

Menuki are decorative metal fittings that cover Mekugi, nail, that secures the handle of the sword to the tang of the blade. The Menuki keeps the Mekugi from slipping out. Eventually they became purely decorative.

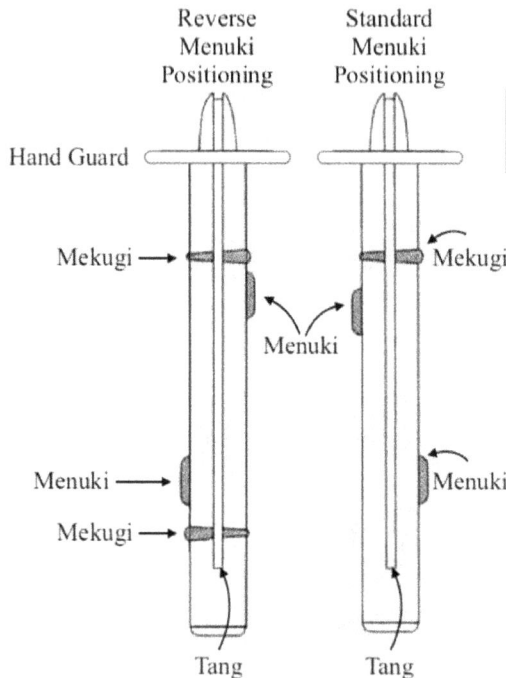

Reverse Menuki Positioning — Standard Menuki Positioning

Hand Guard

Mekugi → ← Mekugi

Menuki

Menuki → ← Menuki

Mekugi →

Tang — Tang

Close Quarters Combat

If you are in a duel and your body makes contact with your opponent's body, then understand that Jujutsu and Torite techniques will not be effective. In that situation, it is best to use Sumo.

Sumo

Sumo began in the era of Emperor Suinin 垂仁天皇 who lived from 69BC ~ 70AD (aged 139) the 11th emperor of Japan. At the time Sumo matches were regular events at court, however the tradition has not continued and these days Sumo matches are not done at court. If you look at old documents you will find that in the previous era even Daimyo, the heads of various Domain, practiced Sumo however nowadays it is only done by low class people.

Kenjutsu Training

Long ago (Sengoku Era) most Kenjutsu Dojo did not do duels. Their training consisted primarily of Kata, training fixed patterns, however nowadays most Dojo focus on Shiai, duels. Kenjutsu training has become very detailed. However, if you only train Kata and do not engage in any training duels, you may be under the mistaken impression that if you execute a Kata exactly you will emerge victorious. Most that think this way will find that a duel does not go the way they think it will.

ほ
く
の
な

人
長
ほ
ど

The training pole looks like this, it is about as tall as a person.

Training Pole

There are some people that will craft a pole about head high and plant it in the ground. This is called a Tsuku, striker. People will then use it for solo training, striking and stabbing it. However since the striker is a dead thing, such training is not particularly useful. If you are not training against a living target, then you are not actually training.[27]

---

[27] It is curious that the author criticizes this training pole, yet includes an illustration of it.

Different Approaches

There are also schools of sword that teach, "No matter how your adversary attacks, respond with this technique." They also say this and that about not allowing yourself to be distracted and the importance of maintaining a clear mind. However, anything can happen when you are suddenly thrust into a combat situation.[28]

Kenjutsu Kata were developed by Sensei somewhat reluctantly since without Kata there would be no way to know how to handle the sword. They can be thought of as a guide to the basics of swordsmanship just as I, Ro, Ha[29] are the first letters learned in calligraphy.

Rank in Sword Schools

You often hear of words Kuketsu, Hiden, Menkyo and Inka in relation to schools of swords.

Kuketsu 口決 Oral Transmission

This is a type of teaching that does not involve writing anything down. It is an orally transmitted lesson. Typically, it is something that you are not able to figure out on your own, but will result in a revelation when told.

Hiden 秘伝 Secret Transmission

While Secret Transmission may seem to be something difficult to teach and a lesson kept strictly within a school, only taught to a select few, it is not that at all. This sort of lesson is only taught to a person deemed capable of understanding it by a teacher. This would apply even if the student in question is the son of the teacher.

---

[28] This sounds like another critique of Takuan Soho's book.
[29] Under the old progression of the Japanese Hiragana alphabet I, Ro, Ha… are the first three letters. "Like learning your A,B,Cs."

The great teacher Confucius said,

The Master said, Shan, my doctrine is that of an all-pervading unity.[30]

His disciple, a man named Tsang, immediately understood this and replied, *Yes.*

By replying with *Yes*, it demonstrated that the disciple had immediately grasped what Confucius was saying. There were other students in attendance and when the great Confucius had departed they asked Tsang,

What did he mean when he said "an all-pervading unity"

Tsang, realizing that the other disciples would not be able to comprehend what Confucius said, replied simply with,

Sincerity and consideration, nothing more.[31]

His answer was two words *Chu-Jo* 忠 恕 sincerity and consideration. The first word was *Chu* 忠 which means that you hold another person as dearly as you hold yourself. The second is *Jo* 恕 which refers to despising a thing you would not wish to be done to you, and realizing that others would despise it as well. Therefore You would not do such a thing. Clearly there is more than one way to interpret the concept *Chu-Jo.* Since Tsang understood that the other disciples would not have been able to comprehend what Confucius was saying, he had no choice but to answer in this way.

In other words, if a person does not have the capacity to understand an answer, the answer will be of no use to them.

---

[30] From *The Analects* 里仁 Li Ren *Propriety and Benevolence* Chapter 15. Translated by James Legge

31 James Legge translated this same passage 忠恕而已 as follows: *The doctrine of our master is to be true to the principles of our nature and the benevolent exercise of them to others,-- this and nothing more.*

The first character *Chu* 忠 refers to duty and the second *Jo* 恕 refers to the benevolent exercise of those duties. The final two 而已 mean "only" or "nothing more."

This same principle applies to understanding the Kuketsu, Oral Teachings, and Hiden, Secret Teachings. The only way to achieve a level that will allow you to understand Oral Teachings and Secret Teachings is through Shugyo, intense training over a long period of time.

Certifications such as Menkyo 免許, License in an Art, and Inka 印可, Certificate of Proficiency, will serve as motivational tools, however no matter what art you receive them in, they do not represent the end of your training in that art. Training is something that continues for your whole life.

There was once a famous Sensei who did not offer any sort of licenses as other schools did.[32] In addition, he would teach the lessons he learned from other schools of sword. Further, his school did not have any Shinmon Seishi, a Written Vow Sworn to a God,[33]

---

[32] Schools would have a progression of ranks leading up to a final "complete transmission" certificate. The names for each rank and the total number varied by school.

[33] *Written Vows Sworn to a God* can come in a variety of forms. One is *Go-oh-ho In* 牛王宝印 They are issued by shrines and temples as Yakuyoke 厄除け protection talismans. *Go-oh* is a stone formed in the gall bladder of cows, a Reiyaku 霊薬 miraculous medicine. *Ho In* means Sacred Mark. The same format is used for making contracts between people and as well as vows not to reveal the secrets of a school. The vow below is from 1702. It is written with "crow writing" with each stroke of the Kanji being a crow.

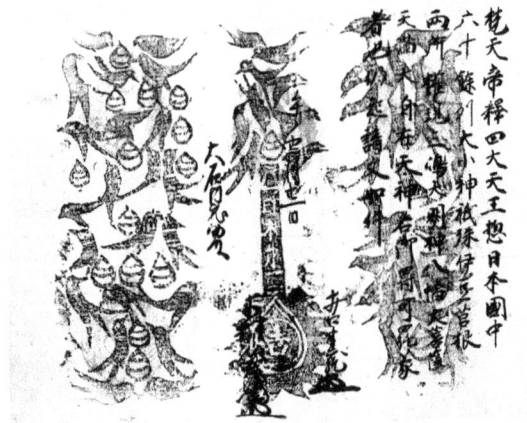

Secret Teachings, or Kuketsu, Oral Teachings. He was a wonderful teacher to learn from.

Long ago in China, when a general was ready to set out for battle, there was a certain ceremony that would be performed. A mound of earth would be built and the lord would seat himself upon it. From atop the ceremonial mound the lord would grant his top general a battle axe. [34] This was a symbol of authority granting the general the right to command his lord's army.

Further, even if the general had to issue a simple order, he would first select an auspicious day to deliver the order and then purify his body in order to ensure even the smallest detail is not neglected.[35]

Some schools have a very simple teaching method while others have a complex, multistep teaching progression. However one is not necessarily better than the other.

Even if there is no one to instruct you in Oral Teachings or Secret teachings, if you devote yourself wholly to training, at some point you will naturally develop an understanding of those teachings. There is nothing more powerful than a person who has developed an understanding of such teachings on their own.

Regarding Training

If you look at the people training in any art you will find people that are deft and people that are clumsy, however any person who devotes their whole mind and body without slacking off will invariably find great success.

There is a saying that goes,

If you see another person execute a technique skillfully once, practice that technique ten times. If you see a person execute a

---

[34] *Ono Masakari/Fuetsu* 斧鉞 Battle axe. This word is two Kanji, both of which mean "axe."
[35] *Saikai-mokuyoku* 斎戒沐浴 Purification of the body including washing as well as fasting and abstaining from sex.

technique skillfully ten times, then you should train that technique a hundred times. [36]

There was once a great teacher that wrote a song about this.

Something you enjoy, something you succeed at and something you become skillful at. Looking at these three things it is clear that you become skillful at something you enjoy.

What this means is that it is important to devote yourself thoroughly to training[37] and not allow yourself to become distracted.

Sword Stances and Attacks

Each Kenjutsu school may have many different types of stances however there are all not so different. Further, while Kenjutsu has ten thousand variations of a thousand possible techniques the attacks are actually limited to Jodan (cutting down from above,) Gedan (cutting up from below,) Joge Naname (cutting diagonally starting either from above or below,) Yoko Ichimonji (cutting horizontally) and Tsuki (straight thrust.)

This is an easy thing to say however developing these skills requires intensive training over a long period of time. When you engage with an adversary if you do not have the ability to move

---

[36] From *The state of equilibrium and harmony* chapter in *The Doctrine of the Mean* 中庸 attributed to Zisi a grandson of Confucius. James Legge's translation of the whole section is as follows:

If another man succeed by one effort, he will use a hundred efforts. If another man succeed by ten efforts, he will use a thousand. Let a man proceed in this way, and, though dull, he will surely become intelligent; though weak, he will surely become strong.

[37] Keiko 稽古 means training, however it is not limited to martial arts. Developing your skills in tea ceremony, calligraphy or pottery is also Keiko, training.

freely and adapt your attacks, it will not matter how fervent your spirit is.[38] Since the second volume of this book will discuss secret teachings related to how to train, I will not write about them here.

You have no doubt heard of techniques like Saya-tome, stopping an attack with the scabbard, Yoji Gakura, throwing a hidden toothpick at a person's eye, as well as things like Kane Shibari, "binding with metal" causing temporary paralysis and Marishiten no Ho, using your fingers to cut a shape in the air to dispel evil and grant protection. Unfortunately, even some well-known Kenjutsu Sensei attempt to deceive students who are lacking in knowledge about this topic. If you are interested in beginning Kenjutsu training I encourage you to be cautious about this.

Long ago there was a Buddhist nun who set out one night. As she was walking, she inadvertently stepped on a frog, killing it. On her way home she was completely dejected, thinking,

I have spent the last ten years living according to the rule that I should never kill a living thing, I am incredibly sad.

When she fell asleep her dreams were plagued by innumerable frogs that admonished her,

Though you are a nun you stepped on and killed one of our fellows, you have violated the law against killing living creatures!

The nun tossed and turned in her sleep as the frogs continued to accuse her of murder. At dawn the next day, she went to the area where she had crushed the frog the night before. She found that the thing she thought had been a frog was actually just a piece of rope. In an instant the nun was overcome with relief and her previous sadness was completely swept away.

This is an example of how your mind can become lost and obsessed with a certain thing. Thus, you should endeavor to remain in Tsune-tsune Kokoro, or an everyday state of mind, not focused on any one thing while at the same time ensuring you are observing events and objects as they truly are.

---

[38] *Yatake Gokoro* 弥猛心 fervent spirit

上段のかまへ

倍小輪三まへいふとの光り

Jodan no Kamae
Upper Stance

This is also referred to colloquially as Ogami Uchi, Hands Clasped in Prayer Cut.

Gedan no Kamae
Lower Stance

上段右斜砕〔ひだめ〕

上段のかまへ
山て右より
秋の肩さき〔へ〕
歩也
俗よ袋肉裳
りけさふよのく

Jodan Migi Shaken
Right Diagonal Strike From Above

From Jodan Kamae swing your sword down diagonally from right to left. The cut should enter the top of your opponent's left shoulder.

This cut is also colloquially referred to as Kesa Giri, Cutting Diagonally Along a Monk's Vestment.[39]

---

[39] A 17th century portrait of Buddhist Monk Kyuzan Soei wearing a Kesa over his left shoulder.

Jodan Hidari Shaken
Left Diagonal Strike From Above

This attack can also be done from the left. Start in Jodan Kamae and then cut diagonally into your opponent's right shoulder cutting down toward his left side.

Gedan Migi Naname
Right Diagonal Strike From Below

This cut is also known colloquially as Age-Kesa, Rising Diagonal Cut Along a Monk's Vestment.

Gedan Hidari Naname
Left Diagonal Strike From Below

This cut is also known colloquially as Age-Kesa, Rising Diagonal Cut Along a Monk's Vestment.

右一文字
胴きりて
いふとめん

Migi Ichimonji
Right Horizontal Cut Like the Kanji for One 一

This cut is also known colloquially as Do-giri, waist cut.

左一文字

Hidari Ichimonji
Left Horizontal Cut Like the Kanji for One 一

This cut is also known colloquially as Do-giri, waist cut.

歌左より我が
たのまへ打ちひと
うけかじし切る
男へ

Uke Nagashi
Block and Pass

Your opponent cuts down in a diagonal right cut, aiming for your left shoulder. This illustration shows how to do an Uke Nagashi, block and pass. After deflecting your opponent's sword, you cut.

Uke Nagashi
Block and Pass

Your opponent cuts down in a diagonal left cut, aiming for your right shoulder. This illustration shows how to do an Uke Nagashi, block and pass. After deflecting your opponent's sword, you cut.

青眼の搆へ

Seigan no Kamae
Clear Eyed Stance

The following topics will be discussed in Book II.

- *Baai No Koto*
  Interval

- *Metsuke*
  Where to Look

- *Chotan no Kane*
  Measuring Length or Shortness

- *Shiai no Kokoro Gake*
  How to Approach Dueling

- *Ki no Atsukai*
  How to Control Your Energy

- *Ki no Okidokoro*
  Where to Place Your Spirit

- *Aiki no Saki*
  When Evenly Matched, Attack First

- Irimi no Kokoroe
  How to Defend Against a Close Quarters Attack

- *Hitori Keiko no Shikata*
  How to Do Solo Training

- *Shinmyo Ken*
  True Mysterious Sword

ERIC SHAHAN

Kenjutsu Hiden Hitori Shugyo
剣術秘伝独修行
Secrets of Japanese Swordfighting
A Guide to Solo Training
Book 2
秘伝
Hiden
Secret Teachings

Japanese Swordfighting: Secrets of Solo Kenjutsu Training
Book 2 : Secret Teachings

Kenjutsu Hiden Hitori Shugyo
剣術秘伝独修行
Secrets of Japanese Swordfighting: A Guide to Solo Training
Book 2

Hiden
Secret Teachings

You have probably heard a saying that goes,

Secrets are like your eyelashes, even though they are above and below your eyes, you can't see them. However, if you look in the mirror they are immediately apparent.

Similarly, there's a secret teachings says,

Pick up a mirror and look at your eyelashes.

If you understand a certain teaching then you do not think anything is difficult about it, however when you are teaching it to a person who has no knowledge of it is called Hiden, transmitting a secret. What follows is what I have learned from what was taught to me by my teacher.

To reach the paradise of the Buddha one must cross the ten-thousand times a hundred million lands that have been enlightened to the word of the Buddha. Another way of thinking of this is Saha, the Land of Eternally Tranquil Light or place where all beings are subject to the cycle of birth and death.[40]

This refers to when you are in a state of are in doubt or are conflicted. Due to this you have moved to an extremely distant plateau, however once becoming enlightened, you won't return to this world rather you will be in a peaceful land of brilliant light without worry confusion and everything will be permanent and immutable.

---

[40] Jumanokudo 十万億土 The innumerable lands between this world and heaven, the pure land. The Shaba-soku-jakkō 娑婆即寂光

As you train sword fighting your teacher will instruct you in Hiden, Secret Teachings. Upon receiving that instruction you should take that lesson and, without doubting it, train it intensely. If you do this that technique will invariably allow you to achieve great success. There is no doubt in that regard. That is why, even when transmitting a seemingly minor teaching, you should ensure your body is purified.[41] For example, in ancient China a general will build a ceremonial mound before handing over the battle-axe to his commander, and thereby authority to kill.[42] This is to ensure that the person receiving the lesson understands its importance.[43]

This next section will detail how to conduct training in Kenjutsu despite not having an instructor or a knowledgeable acquaintance. That being said this is not something to be treated lightly.

Say you were to find a sword instructor, if his lessons only consisted of, "If your opponent attacks like this, respond like this. If your opponent cuts like that, block like this." You will be wholly unprepared to handle yourself in a real duel.

Every person has only two hands so whenever a duel ensues the attacks used are basically the same and this means the duel will not go as you expect. What I am describing is known as Kata Heiho, training using set patterns.

In Kenjutsu you transfer what you feel in your mind to your hands in an instant. Thus, no matter how much Yakusoku Keiko, training with a prescribed attack and a prescribed defense, you do, you will not become skilled. Training according to principles like, "If you do this then respond this way or if your opponent does that then respond that way" are all worthless.

The only way to develop an understanding of sword fighting is to completely dedicate yourself to training. The type of training I am referring to starts in the morning and ends in the evening with your teacher giving instruction throughout. However, many of you do

---

[41] Jojin-Kessai 精進潔斎 This purification includes not only physically cleaning the body but can also include things like abstaining from drinking alcohol, having sex and eating meat.
[42] Presumably building this mound requires a great number of purification rituals.
[43] Soryaku 麁略 half-hearted crudely.

not have access to an instructor or even friends that are knowledgeable about Kenjutsu so this is impossible. However there is a way to train on your own.

For proof of this we can look at how skillful Minamoto Yoshitsune was with the sword. He did not have a Sensei, though some say he was taught by Tengu mountain goblins or by monkeys. One or the other taught Yoshitsune the inner mysteries of the sword arts, however this is likely not a real story.

Though I stated that the story of using a monkey as a training partner was apocryphal, there is an interesting episode regarding just such a situation. A certain person kept a monkey as a pet. He would often try to stab the monkey with his bamboo sword, but the monkey would always leap up or flip to the side, avoiding the blow. Sometimes the monkey would grab the end of the bamboo sword. In short, the man was never able to jab the monkey with his sword. One day however, just as he was attacking the monkey, the scullery maid called out to him with a question. Distracted he grunted, "What?" as he stabbed. This time he struck the monkey with the end of his sword. I think it is important to understand why this occurred.

How to Train on Your Own

When I speak of solo training, I don't think you should spend your time leaping forward and back, then jumping from side to side. That would not be training. Further, planting a training pole in the ground and attacking it is not real training either, since your opponent is a dead thing. The fact is, unless your opponent is a living thing what you are doing will not be training. What you need to do is ask an older or younger sibling, or even some local children, to help you. However, the first two or three times the children will find the activity an interesting amusement. However, they will soon tire of it and refuse to participate anymore.

Long ago in China, when the army was battling nomadic tribes who were invading from the northwest, the Chinese generals found that the nomad's skill at archery far surpassed that of their own soldiers. The generals encourage their soldiers to train with the bow and improve their skills, however most of the soldiers found the training dull and the situation did not improve. However, eventually one general came up with a plan. He developed a target with a certain mark on it. Any soldier who could hit this mark would receive prize money. Soon, all the soldiers became motivated during training sessions and even began practicing on their own. In the end the overall level of archery skill in the Chinese army improved greatly.

Similarly, you should tell the children you gathered, "If you hit me once, I will give you this. If you hit me again, I will give you that." If the prizes are candy, art, a folding fan, or other such items children like, they will participate enthusiastically in your training sessions and you will have motivated opponents to challenge you. Generally speaking, if you are between 18 and 20 years old and you are planning to start solo Kenjutsu training, you should find some children who are about 14 or 15 years old. They should also be smaller and not as strong as you.

A person close to your own age, on the other hand, will be able to strike quite hard, so that is not ideal for beginning training. On the other hand, if your opponent is a child, then even if he hits you, it won't hurt much and you will be able to engage with him easier. The first step is to learn how to cut accurately to Men (the head,) Kote (the hands/forearms) and Do (the midsection) so that you do not injure each other. When you actually begin dueling with your young opponents, you will of course not attack at all, only defend. On the other hand, you should instruct your opponent to cut, strike and stab at you in any way they like. In response to these attacks, you will use Uke, block, or Hazushi, deflection.

When you initially began this training, you will no doubt get struck ten times out of ten duels. However, after several training sessions it will improve to eight losses out of ten. From there you will improve to five or six out of ten before finally you are finally able to avoid being struck in ten out of ten matches. This is the first step in solo training.

Of course, training like this means that you never get to practice attacks, so if you encounter an opponent who is of equal ability, you will not be able to win. Therefore, the next step is to learn the importance of attacking first, before your opponent has time to react. However, you should never aim for a specific target. If you take the time to select your target and strike, a gap will appear in your defenses, which your opponent can capitalize on. Instead, rush headlong in and strike. If you miss, then drop back and attack with a strike to the right or left side of his head. If that too misses, then continue attacking. If you continue to train in this fashion, you will eventually become able to see the gaps in your opponent's defenses.

There is also Goken, Later Sword. Even if your opponent has launched an attack first, you launch your own attack while your opponent's attack is underway. You need to also be training to use Later Sword to meet your opponent's attack and allow it to flow off your blade and then cut.

Ways to Attack

- **_Sen no Sen_**
  Attacking the Moment You See an Opening
- **_Go no Sen_**
  Defending Against an Opponent's Attack, then Attacking.
- **_Sen Go no Sen_**
  Launching Follow-up Attacks After Your Opponent Successfully Blocked Your Initial Attack

When you are facing off against another swordsman and you attack the instant you see his eyes shift in a Kyo, or feint, is called attacking with Sen no Sen, Attacking the Moment You See an Opening. In this scenario there is no Go Ken, After Sword. Your response to your opponent attempting a feint by moving his eyes should be so fast that not even a hair can fit in the interval between his feint and your attack. If you are slow, his Kyo, feint, will lead to Jitsu, his true attack. Again, this interval of time is small enough that even a single hair cannot pass through it.

If your opponent takes the initiative and attacks first, respond with an Uke Nagashi, meeting his blade with your own and allowing it to slide off your sword. Next, do a Kaeshi Gatana, or rotate your sword around and cut. This is known as Go no Sen, Defense and then Attack.

If your opponent responds to your initial attack by blocking with his sword and allowing your blade to slide off and then trying to cut, you have to decide whether to drop back out of his range or do a deflection of your own. This would be Sen Go no Sen, Launching

Follow-up Attacks After Your Opponent Successfully Blocked Your Initial Attack.

Clearly this does not describe every encounter in sword fighting since Kenjutsu consists of a thousand variations of ten thousand techniques. That being said, these names are commonly written down and these general categories are used.[44]

---

[44] Miyamoto Musashi also wrote about this point *in Book of Five Rings*:

Three Approaches to Dueling

There are three approaches to dueling. The first is when you attack your enemy first. This is called Ken no Sen 懸の先 Striking First. The second is waiting for the enemy to attack you before responding. This is called Tai no Sen 待の先, Waiting to Attack.
One more way of dueling is when you launch an attack at your enemy and he attacks you in the same moment. When both of you are attacking at the same time it is called Tai-tai no Saki 躰々の先 Body on Body Attack.

No matter what battle you are in, these are the only three possible initial attacks. Since a battle is typically decided by the first engagement and will enable you to achieve victory. That is why it is the most important lesson in swordfighting. There are of course many other details about the different types of Sen, Initial Encounters, however they are all based on specific situations. It is essential that you see past the surface of your opponent and understand his underlying intent. My way of swordfighting relies on using cleverness in order to achieve victory so I will not add any more details regarding this.

-Book of Five Rings 五輪書 *Fire Scroll* 火の巻
Miyamoto Musashi 宮本武蔵

Baai No Koto
Interval

The word Baai, or Interval, refers to the distance you should maintain between yourself and your opponent.[45] If the interval is too great, then your Katana will not reach your opponent. On the other hand, if you are too close, then you will not have freedom of movement. However, I cannot give you a standard distance to maintain. You can only learn to detect the proper distance to maintain from your opponent through training.

This is known as Suigetsu no Kane, The Ruler Between Moon and Water. The word Suigetsu, means Moonlight Reflected on Water, however this concept refers to the closest distance you can approach your opponent while still being outside his striking range. Another way of referring to this distance is Issoku-Itto no Aida 一足一刀の間, One Step One Cut Distance, meaning you are close enough to your opponent that if you take a step, one or both of you will be in range to cut.[46]

---

[45] Baai 場合 usually means "situation" or "circumstances" however by "situation" the author is clearly referring to distance. The word Maai 間合い or interval/distance, is more common today.

[46] The principle of Suigetsu no Kane is also introduced in the *Heihokadensho* written by sword master Yagyu Munenori (1571~1646.)

Suigetsu no Kane 水月の矩
To be a swordfighter you need to understand Suigetsu no Kane, the Measure Between Moon and Water, meaning the distance you need to position yourself in front of your enemy so that his sword will not strike you.

-Heihokadensho
By Yagyu Munenori
1632

Metsuke
Where to Look

The most important aspect of a duel is where you look. This can decide whether you win or lose a duel. You should be looking into your opponent's eyes. Whatever a person is thinking will show in their eyes.

Mencius said,

Of all the parts of a man's body there is none more excellent than the pupil of the eye. The pupil cannot be used to hide a man's wickedness. If within the breast all be correct, the pupil is bright. If within the breast all be not correct, the pupil is dull. Listen to a man's words and look at the pupil of his eye. How can a man conceal his character?[47]

The same applies to Kenjutsu. The moment your opponent considers an action, it will be apparent in his eyes. Mencius uses the word Boshi 眸子 which refers to the pupil of the eye. You should launch your attack the moment your opponent's pupil moves. This is a Kenjutsu Hiden, a secret teaching of sword fighting and a lesson you should remember. However, if you do not train yourself regularly you will not be able to effectively use this knowledge.

---

[47] Translated by James Legge.

Chotan no Kane
Measuring Length or Shortness

People come in different sizes, so there are long swords and short swords. When you face off against an opponent who is taller than you, you will find that while your Katana cannot reach him, your opponent's sword can strike you powerfully on the head. In this situation you have no choice but to plant your feet firmly and fight him head on. There is a Doka 道歌 Moral Poem, that goes,

Flowing at the end of a great wave. There are rapids where even the horse chestnut shells can float only by abandoning the seed within.

This also applies to the length of your Katana.

Shiai no Kokoro Gake
How to Approach Dueling

The first time you enter a training duel you will no doubt feel as if you are stepping onto the battlefield of a real war. You will feel your heart pounding in your chest. However eventually, after many duels, engaging with opponents will become familiar, and you will begin to think of it as a game. However, it is important to always maintain that first sense of seriousness you had as a beginner. Further, though you may be new to dueling, it is important to face larger, older and more experienced opponents without hesitation. In addition, no matter how powerful your opponent may be, no matter how many victories he may have, you must not fear and dread training with him.

You will find that if you train in a different location, your perspective on training will also change. Further, when training with members of other sword fighting schools, you will find the outcome of your duels are better when you are in your own Dojo than when you go to the Dojo of another school. The latter situation is much more difficult.

Thus, my advice is to try and change the place where you train from time to time. Training with many different people in many different places is the best way to become proficient. If you only duel with the same people over and over again, each swordsman will become well aware of the other swordsman's Kuse, inclinations when fighting, so the duels tend to become formulaic. So I recommend you change training partners and find as many new people to train with as possible. Therefore it is important to duel with members of other schools

While it is important to train with different people and at other Dojo, remember that your objective is training. Do not allow such opportunities to devolve into win-or-lose duels. This will result in losing perspective on what the purpose of intensive training is.

Long ago, there was a thing called Musha Shugyo, Warrior's Training Pilgrimage, where those following the way of the sword would travel to all the domains of Japan, seeking places to train. However, when they trained at another school, they behaved honorably and acted respectfully to all. Since they were requesting permission to train at a school, they would under no circumstances attempt to fight with the members of that school.

In *The Analects* contains the following passage,

The Master said, The student of virtue has no contentions. If it be said he cannot avoid them, shall this be in archery? But he bows complaisantly to his competitors; thus he ascends the hall, descends, and exacts the forfeit of drinking. In his contention, he is still the Junzi.[48]

A Samurai is a man of virtue. The reason he trains in Kenjutsu is to serve his lord and protect his family. Therefore, embarking on a Warrior's Training Pilgrimage is to serve that end and engaging in reckless fighting is counter to that goal.

---

[48] Translated by James Legge.

As Roshi says,

Forasmuch as he will not quarrel, the world will not quarrel with him.[49]

Therefore, even if a person were to pick a fight, you would, out of respect, decline such an offer and not fight. This will cause the other person to feel shame, eventually causing him to respect you. This is the most important thing for a Samurai to remember and should always be at the forefront of your mind.

If you are in a duel with real swords, then the result will be clear to anyone. However, when using bamboo swords people tend to get into debates over whether a hit occurred. Both people who are training know in their hearts what happened. Therefore, even if you are sure that a blow struck your opponent, if he denies it occurred, do not debate it.

There is a Doka, Moral Poem, that goes,

If you ask a man, does a thing exist or doesn't it? He will answer. But if he must ask his heart, he will not have a response.

Ki no Atsukai
How to Control Your Energy

Ki, Energy, is a product of yourself, but you cannot control it freely. While most people will not say this, Shobu-Ki, Your Fighting Spirit and Desire for Victory in Battle, is one of the most important aspects since it will affect how you apply techniques.

---

[49] The Tao Te Ching 道德經 written circa 400 BC and credited to Laozi 老子. The full passage:

Therefore the wise man, embracing unity as he does, will become the world's model. Not pushing himself forward he will become enlightened; not asserting himself he will become distinguished; not boasting of himself he will acquire merit; not approving himself he will endure. **Forasmuch as he will not quarrel, the world will not quarrel with him.**

-Translated by Dwight Goddard (1861~1939)

If you have an open mind and your body is healthy you will be full of vital energy.

Mencius described himself as,

Having a vast flowing passion-nature.

When a student asked what this meant, Mencius responded,

Nothing short of righteousness and justice can satisfy the hunger of the soul.

By staying true to your principles and preserving righteousness, there will be nothing under heaven you must fear. By maintaining this state of mind, you will be able to develop a *"vast, flowing passion-nature."*

Learning Kenjutsu works in the same way. You must train diligently over a long period of time until you have learned techniques correctly and infused them into your body. By training in this manner your body will be filled to overflowing with fighting spirit and you will not need to fear anything.

Ki no Okidokoro
Where to Place Your Spirit

You should place your spirit in Kenbiki Moto,[50] an area between your neck and shoulders.

The fearful chill you get late at night or when gazing down into an abyss is Kenbiki Moto. It also is similar to how foxes and tanuki's transform themselves in order to deceive people. Thus, you should

---

[50] Kenbiki Moto/Kenpeki Moto 痃癖元

痃 cramps

癖 habit or mannerism

元 source

Kenbiki 痃癖 Is an affliction where the muscles from the neck to the shoulder stiffen. Kenpeki Moto is a martial arts term, possibly derived from the same source indicating where the Ki, or spirit, should be maintained and seems to refer to "the base of the neck."

focus your fighting spirit in Kenbiki Moto while your mind should be focused on the spot below your navel. It is often said that you should look with your eyes but see with your belly. This requires you to develop Kufu, a trick of the trade, in order to make it work for you.

This topic is one that requires a lot of training to understand. Even if someone teaches it to you or you read it in a scroll or book you will not be able to comprehend it. You have to regularly train and set your mind to the task of developing this skill until it becomes part of you.

Aiki no Saki
When Evenly Matched, Attack First

A state where the bodies of both you and your opponent are full of vital energy as you face off against each other is known as Aiki, Evenly Matched Energy.

Sun Tsu said,

A clever general, therefore, avoids an army when its spirit is keen[51]

---

[51] From 軍爭 - Maneuvering

*A whole army may be robbed of its spirit; a commander-in-chief may be robbed of his presence of mind. Now a soldier's spirit is keenest in the morning; by noonday it has begun to flag; and in the evening, his mind is bent only on returning to camp. **A clever general, therefore, avoids an army when its spirit is keen**, but attacks it when it is sluggish and inclined to return. This is the art of studying moods.*

Disciplined and calm, to await the appearance of disorder and hubbub amongst the enemy - this is the art of retaining self-possession. To be near the goal while the enemy is still far from it, to wait at ease while the enemy is toiling and struggling, to be well-fed while the enemy is famished - this is the art of husbanding one's strength.

-Translated by Lionel Giles

Thus, it is best to not engage with an enemy that is filled with powerful energy and instead retreat. However, in this situation, withdrawing would mean being pursued and overcome by your opponent. That would mean you would be on the defensive and only able to use Uke Dachi, Blocking Sword, in face of your opponent's vigorous attacks. Being unable to attack will mean you will be defeated. Thus you are in a quandary as you can neither advance nor retreat in this situation. To add to your problem, the space you are training in limits the distance you can move forward or back.

Generally speaking when a swordman is defending he is in a difficult situation. The only solution is to throw caution to the wind and attack with vigor. If you miss, then open up the distance between you and your opponent but continue to cut from the left, right, up and down in a continuous stream of attacks until a Sukima, gap, in the opponent's defenses naturally emerges. Striking that gap in his defenses is called Aiki no Saki, When Evenly Matched, Attack First.

On the other hand, it is essential that you do not allow your opponent to attack you in this manner.

Irimi no Kokoroe
How to Defend Against a Close Quarters Attack

There are many schools of sword that focus on Irimi, Advancing on Your Opponent Until Your Bodies Make Contact. Some of them may use a longer sword, others may use a shorter sword however as soon as their sword makes contact with their opponent's sword, they charge in close. Generally speaking the person who finds themselves on the receiving end of such an attack will lose. When your opponent drives in so close he is right beside you, it is hard for you to attack him with your sword, so you have no choice but to switch to Kumi Uchi, Hand-to-Hand Combat.

That being said, it is difficult to apply Irimi to more than one opponent at a time. Therefore, you do not need to train it to a great degree.

If your opponent is armed with a short Shinai, bamboo sword, and you strike straight to the top of his head, he will simply block your attack and continue his advance.

Therefore, you should cut to either his left or right shoulder or up from below into his left or right armpit. This will counter the attack of an opponent armed with a short Shinai.

In addition, swordsman that excel at Irimi techniques tend to have a limited repertoire of techniques.

If your sword and your opponent's sword are of equal lengths then the duel will come down to who has learned more techniques. Both opponent's in a duel having Shinai, Bamboo Swords, of equal lengths is known as Aisun, Matching Lengths.

Swordsmen that excel at Irimi tend to use Seigan Stance, Gedan Stance or Naname Diagonal Stance. This topic is something that must be made part of your regular training.

Hitori Keiko no Shikata
How to Do Solo Training

Earlier, I described how to conduct intensive training on your own. Find some local children and have them attack you. When you have developed some techniques, find some opponents closer in age to yourself. If you only train with opponents weaker than yourself then you will not be able to apply techniques effectively. The best idea is to try and gradually find larger and stronger opponents.

This does not apply just to Kenjutsu but any art. The lessons that your teacher passes onto you are the fundamentals, so the movements are prescribed. In order to become able to respond to any of the myriad movements a real adversary is capable of means you have to develop a new technique each time you are exposed to a new opponent. Your teacher instructing you in how to respond will not result in those techniques becoming part of you.

Ishin-denshin, describes a state where the person being taught understands the lesson without the person teaching having to say anything. Further, without speaking, the person teaching realizes the student understands. Thus while you may have a Sensei or you may not, the ability to understand the ultimate in Kenjutsu remains because in the end you are training on your own. This concept is something you should consider carefully.

Shinmyo Ken
True Mysterious Sword

Every Kenjutsu school has a secret sword technique called Shinmyo Ken. When you are set to receive such a lesson, you must first purify your body and exhibit the highest level of manners and respect to your teacher. There is no situation where this would be taught in a casual manner. If you do not approach receiving this lesson with the upmost sincerity, it is highly likely you will not be able to fully grasp what is being taught. Thus, there would be no reason to pass such a lesson onto you. Though you are likely be nervous, you should listen to your Sensei with the upmost care.

While I am hesitant to write the following passage, I understand there are those that live in remote areas without any chance to train with a proper instructor or a knowledgeable friend. Since these people are endeavoring to learn Kenjutsu and I am writing a book about how to train conduct solo sword training, I will record some information about True Mysterious Sword.

I am only teaching this to those of you reading this book and it is not something you should ever talk about to another person.

The word Shinmyo Ken is comprised of three Kanji. The first, Shin, refers to something completely true without a hint of falsehood or decoration. The second is Myo, which refers to something mysterious and miraculous done by a god. Something no one can predict and no one can describe. In other words, something that can only be felt in the mind understood by the mind and will naturally cause your body and limbs to move. The third is Ken, meaning sword.

There is a Doka, Moral Poem that goes,

The Kanji Myo is like the tousled hair of a young girl, saying something or not saying something, brushing or not brushing.
Tying it up or not tying it up, explaining or not explaining.[52]

However True Mysterious Sword is neither the special name of a sword nor the name of a technique. It is not something that will cause your level of skill to rise upon hearing it. Rather, after a long period of dedicated training you will come to a realization. "Ah, this is what is meant by Shinmyo Ken, True Mysterious Sword!" This is a "famous sword" that must be kept secret.

I will give an example that will allow beginners to understand, please read the following lines carefully.

Image that two combatants are brimming with fighting spirt. They attack each other ferociously, though neither can land a blow. However, an opening appears in one warrior's defenses. This opening is barely a moment long. It exists for an interval of time so small not even a single hair can fit through. However, your blade finds this gap due to your years of dedicated training. You have reacted as fast as the spark given off by steel striking stone. This is Shinmyo Ken.

What this means is you are not thinking of what technique you are going to apply or how you will approach your opponent. In addition, this does not describe a lucky strike either, as it would be impossible to land a blow like that on a skilled opponent.

Sekka, striking steel on stone to produce a spark. The moment the steel hits the stone, a spark flies out. There is no interval between the stone being struck and the spark emerging. This is what is meant by "reacting to an opening so small not even a hair can fit in." This is not something that can occur by chance.

---

[52] 妙の字は若き女のみだれ髪ゆふにゆわれずとくにとかれず
Due to the many homophones in Japanese the second line of this poem could mean either:
"saying something or not saying something, brushing or not brushing."
or
"Tying it up or not tying it up, explaining or not explaining."

Further, as you organize your thoughts before doing something remember the sacred words,

When someone looks at me, it is as if they are seeing to the depths of my being. [53]

In other words, your opponent will be able to completely read your intent. Thus Shinmyo Ken is a lesson to be thankful for. I pray that dedicated practitioners diligently review this lesson and make it part of themselves.

Conclusion

As for myself, from a young age I was interested by Kenjutsu though I cannot say I thought about it day and night. My household was a poor one and thus I had no chance to learn directly from a sword instructor and for the most part I spent my days working at my profession trying to stay ahead. However, as I entered middle age, I was able to find a man who would instruct me and I pursued Kenjutsu with vigor.

Those days went by quickly and now I find that I am an old man of seventy-two years who needs a cane in order to get about. Thus, I was forced to abandon martial arts training. The time I spent

---

[53] This is from *Great Learning*, the first chapter of which is attributed to Confucius with the remaining chapters attributed to his disciple Zengzi. James Legge translated the whole passage as follows:

There is no evil to which the mean man, dwelling retired, will not proceed, but when he sees a superior man, he instantly tries to disguise himself, concealing his evil, and displaying what is good. The other beholds him, as if he saw his heart and reins;— of what use is his disguise? This is an instance of the saying—"What truly is within will be manifested without." Therefore, the superior man must be watchful over himself when he is alone.

Zengzi's Sixth Commentary
"On having the thoughts sincere."
-Translated by James Legge

training was short, so I have no intention of speaking of this art in a grand manner.

Long ago there was a Sensei who said he could teach the secret of eternal life and eternal youth. A great many students joined his classes and many learned his secret method. However that Sensei who taught the secret of eternal life and eternal youth died suddenly one day. The moral of this story is not that the Sensei lied about what he taught it is that no matter how well you are able to teach something, some people are not able to fully absorb it into their bodies and make it their own.

Thus, despite the fact that I have written this book, please do not think that I am in any way an expert.

Published Kansei 11 (1799)
Republished Kansei 12 (1800)

ERIC SHAHAN

This is the end of the reprint which begins at the end of this book and proceeds right to left.

寛政十一年未十一月御免

同十二年申正月新刑

皇都書肆

寺町通五條上ル甼

岩瀬儀兵衞

巻之下大尾

串と合とをくて実と秘そぎの名詞りくなふ
るの一とにりがぐ神んの人ことありに能く参ん
新ぐし
たらくいバ双をとあい楊に頂熱一番よりて丁くと
打合とくひとのの形りを不と同小盤とく連
ぞ佛林の詞のありうろうす乙火のおちきい真の去
如調なるを敵とれとも乞たもひきてけど又
偶中ふもいうろぐる由くれとも乞とうくゆう去
わさいぐるく乙火とは縁とべくんとくそ
たりもち火の出るとふ孫とくの
火の出るいるふ鞍といれぢるの勢いなり偶中

真言は偽かざり。しく悉く真実ある力とひふゆへに

弁々々々がふかふしてその多くして文練をとろく

伝え不金んんと坊く解悟一自覚こ子べ小義

ぎ多とい小飲小

妙乃宗を坊き女のらうれん發

米いいまどらふられを

けずめく會へずきせられんども真妙詞こ

い々々組の名ふもりし又鉤衝の形もそ

ど伝披しれびめ忽上もする々くも形

像妹功に、とろて媛小古重ぞ真妙詞せらを以

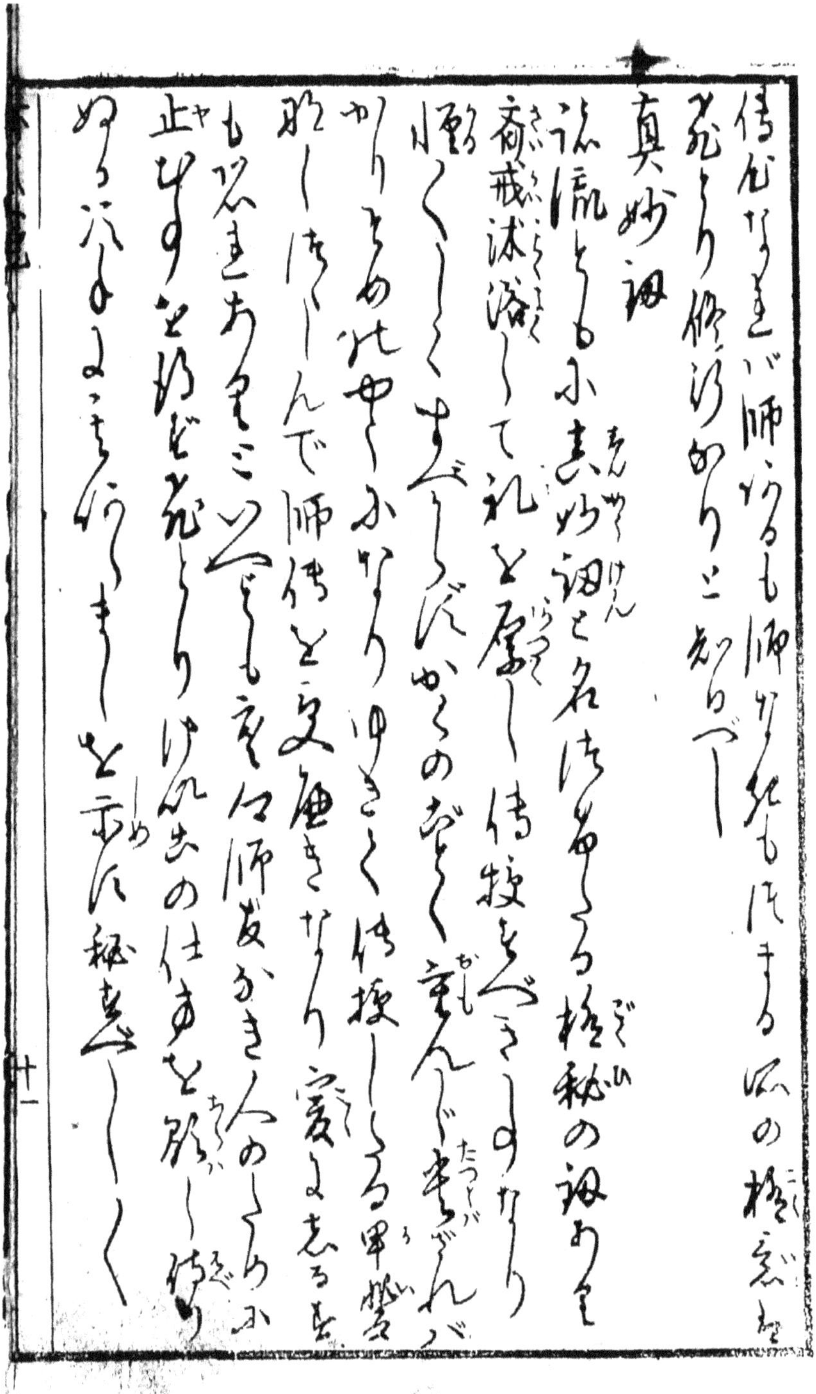

一 真妙調

入身の心持

左者
上ト

下ノ巻

双方体氣満くこ〜て立両ひ〜るいれ氣〜り
孫子ニ云く鋭く〜野ふ〜の八鋭氣と避こ〜れ〜
さくべうのれ〜〜もよく付〜〜ぬ出〜て
け〜〜うけ〜力をかりてよと出たよう〜た
かんところ〜いんも〜さやり〜坊れ〜
もの〜（勢古嫡セ海ち〜も〜進退〜自中せ〜〜ど
こ〜く細がいうる時い損あり男ひ如く〜〜
ふなを打さんで付て〜どは引〜てい〜
〜とぴ〜らくと打立バかの付〜〜遠ら〜〜
べ〜を打とれ氣のせんとつふ却く〜〜ふ
かくのおそく世〜〜事なり〜し

九

氣もものおしく修行功につもり我ふ正しき働
とのまハ休氣まんくらて氣ぐるゝ

氣の垂ふ

氣乃主不ら歡癖とし深又ハ深湖上のぞき
ぐろさもるもけんむきもなるて狐狸小袋ハ
きこ氣と疳癖とふまいつろんハ脇下も垂と
うこと目ふくたしし股よくえろとふす
あり工夫とゝ一切ハ修り功にとげれハ
志まふしゝゞ口伝書ゆふく八合長ゆくふ
いゝゞぞ能くん能く自ゆを書けり

われ氣の光

きうり欲し

人をいたはるとせ、さるべきが

なきことて、おくとさくん

氣乃あれい

氣を我が、よめりんどき、自由ふゆり、べば浩頼

宇一篇にほはいくども業小ゆらりて、いおとりの

かならそのるり心よろく体ゆきっせる八氣此

濱くことりくるを童子浩然の氣と、て紀く

義を道、ふらうてゆきすなうとこの残す

道小たゞっぱ義とき、しいは天下こたようべき

このろーー芯浩然の氣のやーなひらり級

けん太坂〳〵きてハ仕ざりきゝよのりり扔く
瑞而とうそけいに志か〵
月〳〵人〳〵たびく仕合をもちられハ立ふよ解と
初ら曲〳〵仕うきゝよのりゝ立をり
こけんおもろがうゝしゝゝ人少〵たゝゝく仙流と
出合く仕合〳〵つきゝよのりゝまどゝゝ入り大坊
いふすとわろんく譽ひふぞりゝよの〵
兎等ゝ八修りの中志と初〳〵ざるゝを志ら
事りりむ〳〵八武志修行をく法囚とゝろ
ゝゝうらうゝ化流に仕合をちゝも誰意と
すゝく礼義とりつろ〵必ぞわゝよゝふべゝだ

仕合の心持

長柄乃柄

以小長柄

場合之事

場合と云ものは敵に立向ひたるとき、いづれも
をれば右刀ちらぐびとられ、ぐるろ、
自由なりしもへなぐいふす、置く定めやし
なく、立合く自然小合をゆくべきものを卷と

松月の姿こと

目付

仕合の猶頂小寸こともる、目の法を取わり
目付はあり不い眼中切ばんりもり、不肌中
りつゝる童子よなぶ手人共菜良於睯子睯
不肌掩其悪こつゝ命術もまく志らんの

又、懸かること先の先を取りてよきことなれども

先く懸く先く懸くの大事

たびたび立向ふくらべさえゆる不の虚へ

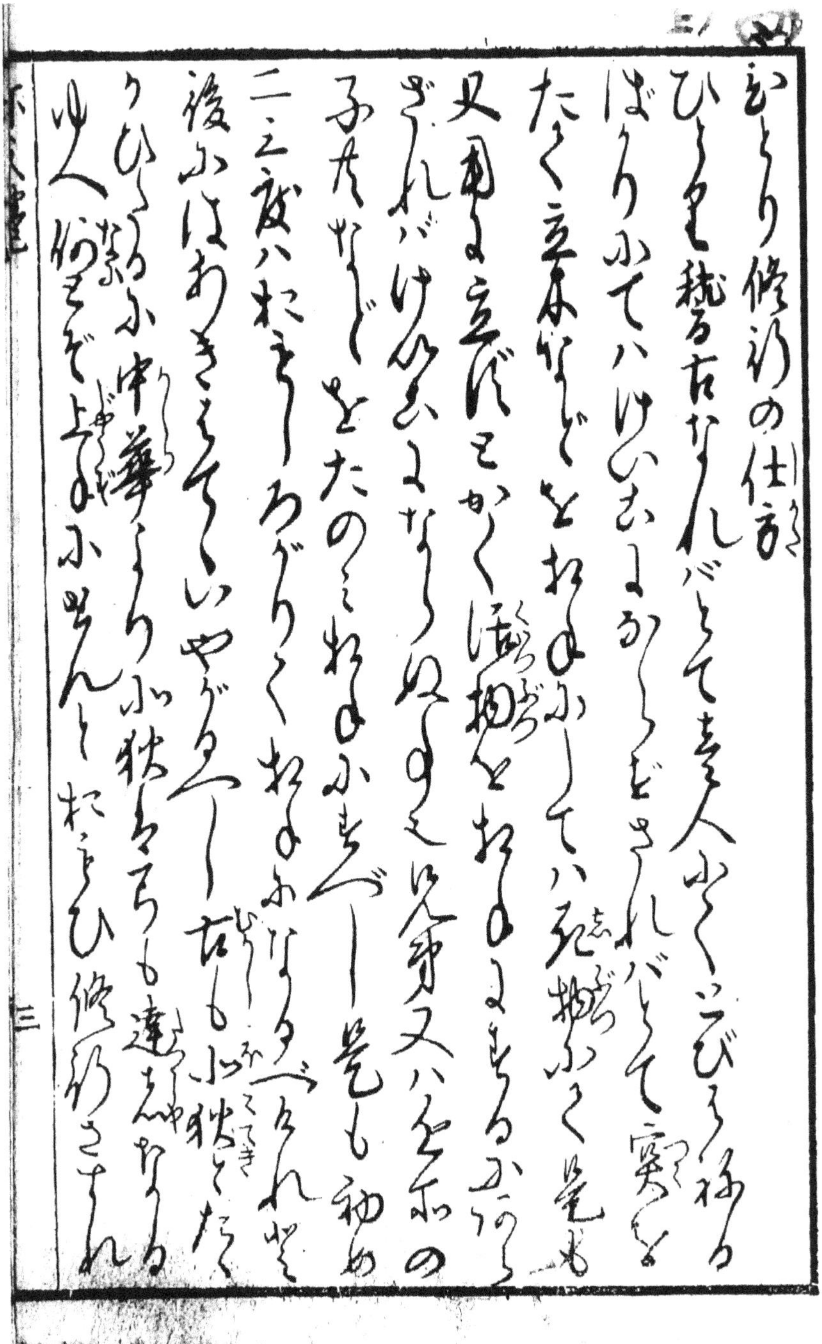

劍術秘傳獨修行巻之下

一秘傳

世の諺小秘事ハ瞳そいふおそく瞳を目の像に沿ひ

に今龍殺生戒と破りくらするの僧し

おとひ給ひて底するのゑ小投多れ

方すく戒と錯殺し殺生戒と犯し

比丘と養くり夜けぬく他の不よゆて

うろてくくれ縄りを熟そけて他の

うるか船が此の甚ひより錘ら不り

理とかしるに支くきろうけも

十六

青眼の搆

歌 右より我が
たのむへ切むと
うけかじて切る
別に

左一文字

右一文字

胴きつて

ふとのん

上段右斜め

上段のかまへ
山て左より
敵の肩さき〔へ〕
寸地
俗よ袋肌
りけ〵ふ〻の〳

下段の搆

上段のかまへ

居小縄を寸をいふとの色へ

嫡範　ねらひ我より間とつむ

目付
附就

長範の矩

仕合んせん

氣れいうつひ

拳乃壺両

れ氣の先

入身れんね

ぬらう修行の仕方

真妙初

右下巻秘傳し龍小記と

に変秘伝と云ゞとも修行功ほうれバ自然ふ
自功をふ猶けるタゞ一自得わど丈夫けりすハ
わ一
法説とも小聖用無里用あ里ゞとも致そうく
勤て怠らざるとの終よき道と林鐘を人つ吾
して錬とんしバ己古里とたうびを人十うびして
錬すまゝぱ己あれと面うびをとうつゝ里大師乃
出欲ふし
皆ゞ功上一〇そ三ッとくゝがれは
すきらゝれ抽乃上もしくいなりゝ
こく退屈せだゝして励ほうむうりゝ

人ふりつうぎまにハ盖ろて
よありて知ろく一　必竟ハ变秘伝各修り
いげまに此藝も毫までありこふか免許印可も勵の一
の動こ或名先生門人ふ於一更に此儘のごく
許可こつふすなく先生ハ一ぱを屬奏にくれま
神文もこうふこふふするもりふりて
こうく更よりがつき翻御乃大道師に稱をじ
されても右こも大ぬく作ぐかた壇と藝き茶鋺と
授くまんどうこ一此事城侍ふ心ふ
齊戒沐浴のうふく吉日良辰とそふふす
道と靈どくめんこ一偏ふ心論じやこ

吾が道一以て之を貫くと曾子い
玄不合点して唯くと答て曾子い
玄をいふ返答之がかも同じやうにいふ唯く八遍よの
ばくて孔子の玄塾と立退ひていろ跡かく今れ一
玄く大玄と貫くに作をいひ何の事ぞと鷄
いろ丞真合点の如くにすぐにと断りて右然のく
なりいろ答てい玄這は他人の事をも玄が
事乃如くかいも如玉りくすりと云想に玄あが
これいりいふ人をいやかりん玄思ひ玉りて過ぐる
いふ玄んしとも右然にいぼつふうらい玄止らせと
ざりの答していひ云秘伝にいぶもからのぎろいて合玄れ

又歌といふものをするは此の刀一むきと言へる
流義によりて安心の堅固をして絶へず修し且つ
猶稽古よかりて八め何なりけんか
すべて形といふものは止すと言はざるより役する
ものおく形はあらざればへ坐きて心せられつべ
叙術乃全躰のそろ若人のいろはヽ
世の中の変秘傳免許印下と言ふれすも書に
き記さべてヽて調ふく教ゆものと記付にすも
合点をる也姫傳さて小さ根ふ者
してはヽれふ事の中やヽまざもたれ共なりぞ
言人ふあらヽざれバ子孫これを修てヽて孔子の

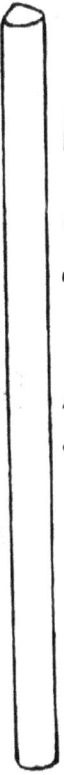

巫覡の小まは虎鞴小撥つく虎乃巻と

罷うり文鞴武鞴虎鞴豹鞴犬鞴と云鞴と云

義経の兵書と見一巻服より

...

淳ふんてうる句術も身の恨りも主、鍛傷らぢ

習惯といり鉄桟に雪めき、孝ふわら〜ぢ三宵

ものあって雪筆と運くする、武藝と學ふふよ主

明の威軌塘も鉤術と多主一ば肝をくゐ主

ら鳥鸞雅力鉤術ろと武士乃寶き藝也

こいぞもうりと一翅いへた一かて常ふ

身ふ藝するそのりれバヤ一ふれミことるよ

鉤術けらて

元来武氏を戈と止りこ本るろ文字ありま主バ學び

立く生雁男立め寅に武道寅加の武士を稗

きゐ一乱り主りと浴矢幕虐と語り平らぎ

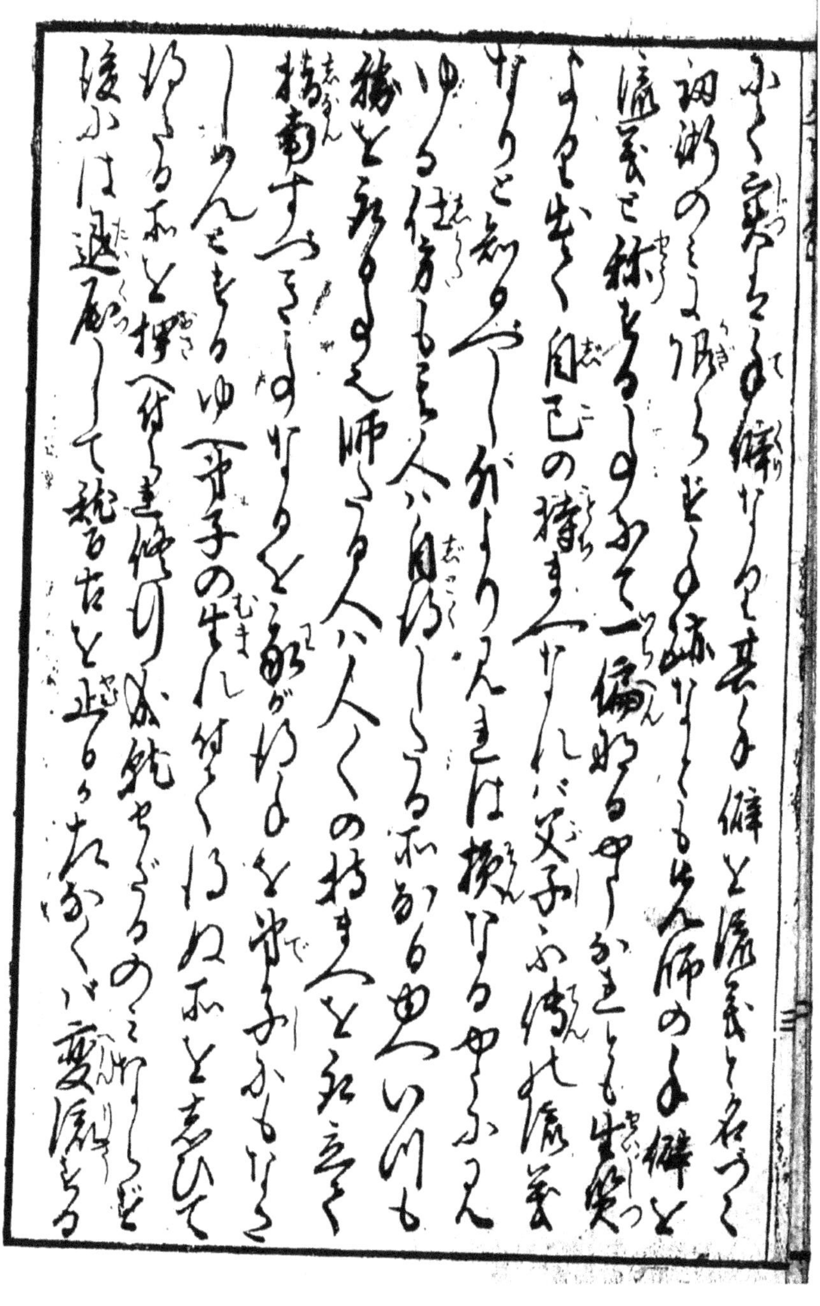

劍術秘傳獨修行卷之上
總論

東都　舊園述

劍術が流行あり其え祖いぢ至も名人ゆりて一血...

此謂父子不傳也是以每人有一流譬
如人面之同而各異也此其姓ノ所以
異於彼役其好之效以傳之彼非所有
而傳之終身不成也嗚呼感乱姓者不
可矯也惟能任橫不蕩於外其行全矣
名之曰獨修行月

寛政戌午之初冬舊園謹識

帰一堂主人衣

自序

或雑曰古人有謂也人非生而知之者

不渉師其為惑終不解矣諸藝皆然矣

而子禪褶修行者豈因随乎平于對曰物

故有未屋推求其来歴即善也矣至于

苦不生有而森羅萬像不可得而觀也

卽術之淪支流多瓢則其業浸而于

萬別而其本一也一者即因有云云